THE QUINTESSENTIAL
PORCINE HISTORY
OF PHILOSOPHY AND RELIGION

THE QUINTESSENTIAL
PORCINE HISTORY
OF PHILOSOPHY AND RELIGION

JAMES TAYLOR

Abingdon Press
Nashville

THE QUINTESSENTIAL PORCINE HISTORY OF
PHILOSOPHY AND RELIGION

ISBN   978-1-4267-5475-3

12 13 14 15 16 17 18 19 20 21—10 9 8 7 6 5 4 3 2 1
MANUFACTURED IN THE UNITED STATES OF AMERICA

CONTENTS

FOREWORD

LET US NOW PRAISE FAMOUS PIGS

"I like pigs," said Churchill. "Dogs look up to us. Cats look down on us. Pigs treat us as equals." Pondering James Taylor's *Quintessential Porcine History*, one realizes the deep religious resonance of man with sow, of *Sus* and Susan.

Take, for instance, the Apollonian Pig—nestled among his tomes, studiously content in the day's small hour. To what do that lowered eyebrow and partial smile advert? Admiration of a well-wrought argument? Perhaps, though I doubt it. He daydreams of the Dionysian bacchanal with his fetching gilt. Who among us has not thrilled to Hooker's *Ecclesiastical Polity* as the Puseyite porker in these pages? Does not the heart of even the most willowy supermodel beat to Feuerbach's rhythm? You bet your trough it does.

Time and again this artist demonstrates a perspicacity rare among theologians. With the subtlest adjustment of line, he captures the surprising sympathy of Pelagian with Augustinian, of Arminian with Calvinist, of the Liberationist and the Evangelical with the Postmodernist. For every swine, much on which to dine.

Admittedly, there are missed opportunities. The most conspicuous omission: Abbot Anthony of the Desert, patron of swineherds, venerated for his miraculous poultice of ham fat. One yearns for Taylor's depiction of that dramatic moment when, during a Kirk session, the wife of Geneva's mayor addressed Calvin as a lying hog. Absent also is the episode recounted in Bernard of Clairvaux's *Life of Malachy of Armagh* (4.8): "When the saint put his finger into each of [a deaf person's] ears, he felt two little things like piglets come out of them. For these and other such deeds, . . . Scots and Irish converged on [Malachy], and he was revered by all as father of both." Would that Taylor's pen had been applied to this wonder, which tells all of Angus and Paddy you'll ever need to know.

These, however, are mild grunts. "It is better," J. S. Mill claimed, "to be a human being dissatisfied than a pig satisfied." Poor Johnny Stu could not have been more confused, as a glance at the slumbering Kantian pig will verify. Luther knew better: "In the street or on its dung-heap, the pig imagines itself on a soft bed: it rests peacefully, snores delicately, sleeps deliciously." The serenity of the Missouri Synod suid, the anguish of the Bergsonian boar, the shoat afloat Kierkegaard's leap of faith—no illustrator could better Mr. Taylor's witty line. Celebrate the return of all these porcine prodigals, and find yourself among them. You're in here, somewhere. I'm the suckling sucking a Granny Smith at the Methodist luau.

C. CLIFTON BLACK
Princeton, New Jersey

I.
Classic Greek Pigs

STOIC PIG

Epicurean Pig

APOLLONIAN PIG

Dionysian Pigs

SIMPLISTIC HEDONIST PIG RISING
ON A MORNING AFTER, TO SERVE
AS AN OBJECT LESSON TO MORE
MODERATE PIGS EVERYWHERE

FOLLOWER OF DEMOCRITUS WHO HAS
JUST CONSUMED A QUANTITY OF
PARTICULARLY SMOOTH ATOMS

ANTI-HERACLITEAN PIG
ATTEMPTING TO STEP INTO
THE SAME STREAM TWICE

RECENT CONVERT TO THALES'
DOCTRINE, "ALL IS WATER."

ENTERPRISING FOLLOWER OF XENO ATTEMPTING TO MAKE HIMSELF RICH BY BETTING ON A RACE HE HAS JUST "ARRANGED"

SOCRATIC PIG AND YOUTHFUL DISCIPLE IN DIALOGUE

Aristotelian Pig
contemplating acorn

**ARISTOTELIAN PIG PREPARING
TO DISTRIBUTE A MIDDLE TERM**

II.
PIGS OF THE ANCIENT AND MEDIEVAL CHURCH

AUGUSTINIAN PIGS SINNING
BECAUSE OF THEIR FALLEN NATURE

PELAGIAN PIGS SINNING JUST BECAUSE THEY WANT TO

Pseudo-Dionysian Pig
Contemplating the Nine Orders of Angels

BOETHIAN PIG BEING CONSOLED BY PHILOSOPHY

REALIST PIG AND NOMINALIST PIG
CONSIDERING EAR OF CORN

OCKHAMIST PIG PONDERING MEANS OF EXAMINING PHILOSOPHICAL ASSERTIONS

PIG IN DEEP PERPLEXITY BECAUSE
HE CAN'T RECALL THE NAME OF
THE BOOK BY MAIMONIDES HE WAS
SUPPOSED TO LOOK UP

ABELARDIAN PIG RESOLVING A YES AND NO QUESTION

Franciscan Pig and congregation

III.
PROTESTANT PIGS

LUTHERAN PIG DEALING
WITH ADVERSARY

**ARMINIAN PIG BEING SAVED
BECAUSE HE FREELY ACCEPTED
THE GRACE OF GOD**

**CALVINIST PIG BEING SAVED BECAUSE
HE IS PREDESTINED TO BE AMONG
THE ELECT**

ANGLICAN PIG GLORYING IN ONE
OF THE MORE PROVOCATIVE
PASSAGES OF **HOOKER'S** *LAWS OF
ECCLESIASTICAL POLITY*

ORTHODOX PRESBYTERIAN PIG
LOOKING FOR SIGNS OF
GRACE REVEALED

ANGLICAN PIG FOLLOWING THE *VIA MEDIA*

Puritan Pig disapproving of something

PURITAN PIG STRIVING TO MAKE HIS ELECTION SURE

METHODIST PIG WHOSE HEART HAS BEEN STRANGELY WARMED

Little band of Methodist Pigs
fleeing from the wrath to come

CAMPBELLITE PIG BEING SILENT WHERE THE BIBLE IS SILENT

IV.
MODERN PHILOSOPHICAL PIGS

Particularly naïve Leibnizian Pig
doing research on monads

NOVICE CARTESIAN PIG TRYING TO FIGURE OUT WHERE HE WENT WRONG

LEIBNIZIAN PIG PONDERING
THE DESIGN OF THE UNIVERSE

Rousseauean Pig encountering a noble savage

BERKELEIAN PIG
NOT BEING PERCEIVED

HUMEAN PIG DEVELOPING
A CRITICISM OF THE ARGUMENT
FROM DESIGN

KANTIAN PIG PRIOR TO AWAKENING
FROM HIS DOGMATIC SLUMBERS

KANTIAN PIG CONTEMPLATING THE STARRY HEAVEN ABOVE AND THE MORAL LAW WITHIN

KANTIAN PIG REFUSING TO LIE TO A MANIAC WHO HAS ASKED THE WHEREABOUTS OF HIS FRIEND

KIERKEGAARDIAN PIG
DEMONSTRATING A LEAP OF FAITH

HEGELIAN PIG OBSERVING A THETICAL PIG AND AN ANTITHETICAL PIG ARRIVING AT A SYNTHESIS

ENTHUSIASTIC CONVERT TO FEUERBACH'S DOCTRINE, "DER MENSCH IST WAS ER ISST."

KIERKEGAARDIAN PIG TRYING TO UNDERSTAND ABRAHAM

V.
TWENTIETH- AND
TWENTY-FIRST CENTURY PIGS

NIETZSCHEAN SUPERPIG

SOMETIMES A CIGAR IS JUST A CIGAR...

FREUDIAN PIG

A FOLLOWER OF **R**UDOLF **O**TTO
EXPERIENCING THE *MYSTERIUM*
TREMENDUM

BARTHIAN PIG

BERGSONIAN PIG ABOUT TO HAVE AN
IDEA THAT NEVER EXISTED BEFORE

EXISTENTIALIST PIG WITH AN ACUTE CASE OF *ANGST*

Two Sartrian Pigs in the days of the Resistance

**BONHOEFFERIAN AND SARTRIAN PIGS
ARGUING OVER WHETHER WHAT THEIR
COMPANION HAS JUST DONE AROSE
FROM CHEAP GRACE OR BAD FAITH**

LOGICAL POSITIVIST PIG
DEVELOPING AN INFORMAL LIST
OF EMOTIVE TERMS

NIEBUHRIAN PIG ATTEMPTING TO REALIZE LOVE AND JUSTICE IN A CONTINUOUS DIALECTIC

TILLICHIAN PIG BECOMING FRUSTRATED IN HIS EFFORTS TO DETERMINE WHICH OF HIS CONCERNS IS ULTIMATE

TEILHARDIAN PIG DEJECTED BECAUSE THE
GREAT JESUIT NEVER PRODUCED WHAT
WOULD HAVE BEEN HIS CROWNING WORK,
THE PHENOMENON OF PIG

Ordinary Language Pig
DOING RESEARCH

SITUATION ETHICS PIG AND
PRINCIPLES ETHICS PIG DISCUSSING
THE NATURE OF CHRISTIAN LOVE

Missouri Synod Lutheran Pig
Caught Up in the Heat
of Ecumenical Fervor

SOUTHERN BAPTIST PIG

SOUTHERN BAPTIST PIGS RECEIVING LATEST UPDATE ON WHAT THEY BELIEVE ABOUT THE SCRIPTURES

UNITED METHODIST PIG GOING OUT TO EXPLAIN TO THE WORLD WHAT THE WORD "UNITED" SIGNIFIES

W**OEFULLY** **INEXPERIENCED** **GROUP** **OF**
L**IBERATIONIST** P**IGS** **WHO** **HAVE** **JUST**
ESTABLISHED **A** **BASS** **COMMUNITY** **AND** **NOW**
ARE **WONDERING** **WHAT** **TO** **DO** **NEXT**

LIBERATIONIST PIG TRYING TO FIGURE OUT WHY
IT'S SO MUCH EASIER TO TALK WITH HIS FRIEND
THE CATHOLIC PIG THAN WITH CERTAIN OTHER
PIGS IN HIS OWN MAINLINE DENOMINATION

EVANGELICAL PIG TRYING TO FIGURE OUT WHY
IT'S SO MUCH EASIER TO TALK WITH HIS FRIEND
THE BAPTIST PIG THAN WITH CERTAIN OTHER
PIGS IN HIS OWN MAINLINE DENOMINATION

POSTMODERNIST PIG TRYING
TO FIGURE OUT WHY IT'S SO HARD
TO TALK WITH ANYBODY AT ALL

MORALIST PIG PONDERING
A STRAIGHTFORWARD DECISION

MORALIST PIG PONDERING AN AMBIGUOUS DECISION

DECONSTRUCTIONIST PIG
INTERPRETING A TEXT

MORMON PIG

Mega-Church Pastor Pigs

HEAR ME ROAR!

FEMINIST PIG

UNIVERSALIST PIG

Post-Denominational Pig

EMERGENT PIG

Mega-Church Pastor Pig

SPIRITUAL-BUT-NOT-RELIGIOUS PIG

POSTMODERNIST PIG

Pig who has found all the answers

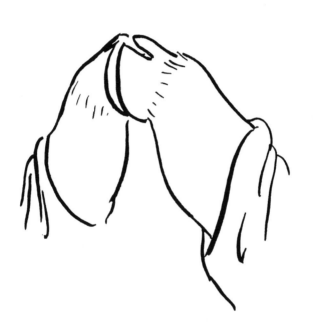